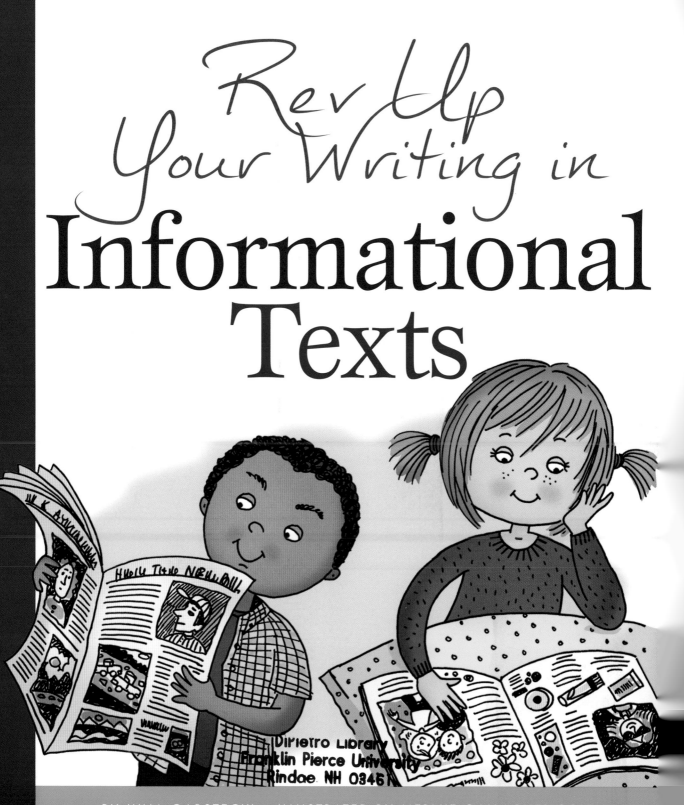

Rev Up Your Writing in Informational Texts

BY JULIA GARSTECKI • ILLUSTRATED BY MERNIE GALLAGHER-COLE

The Child's World

Published by The Child's World®
1980 Lookout Drive • Mankato, MN 56003-1705
800-599-READ • www.childsworld.com

ACKNOWLEDGMENTS
The Child's World®: Mary Berendes, Publishing Director
Red Line Editorial: Editorial direction and production
The Design Lab: Design

PHOTOGRAPHS ©: Dmytro Vietrov/Shutterstock Images,
6; Mariia Mykhaliuk/Shutterstock Images, 12; Samuel
Borges/Shutterstock Images, 18

ISBN 9781634070638
LCCN 2014959941

Printed in the United States of America
Mankato, MN
July, 2015
PA02261

ABOUT THE AUTHOR

Julia Garstecki loves writing. She usually writes for children, but sometimes she writes for parents. Julia started writing when she was in third grade and has not stopped. Her basement is full of stories she has written over the years!

ABOUT THE ILLUSTRATOR

Mernie Gallagher-Cole is a children's book illustrator living in West Chester, Pennsylvania. She loves drawing every day. Her illustrations can also be found on greeting cards, puzzles, e-books, and educational apps.

Table of Contents

CHAPTER ONE

What Is an Informational Text?. 4

CHAPTER TWO

Introductions and Conclusions 10

CHAPTER THREE

Body Paragraphs 16

Tips for Young Writers. *22*
Glossary. *23*
To Learn More *24*
Index. *24*

What Is an Informational Text?

H ave you ever read a book about your favorite animal? Have you read a magazine article about an athlete? Have you learned about an event by reading the newspaper? These are all examples of informational texts.

Informational texts give facts and details. They are about a **nonfiction** topic. This type of writing teaches the reader something new. Sometimes students need to write an essay to answer a question. In this case, an informational text shows what the writer knows.

There are many types of informational texts. Newspapers describe events that just happened. Books teach readers about many things, such as history and science. Brochures tell visitors what they can do on a trip.

Informational texts often have extra features. These things help the reader. Headings tell what each section is about. Pictures show examples. The **glossary** teaches new words. The **index** tells where to find each topic.

In school, most of your writing will explain something you learned. This type of informational text usually has three parts. The **introduction** tells what your reader will learn. **Body** paragraphs give details and examples. The **conclusion** sums up important facts.

You must organize your text. Think about what your readers need to know. For example, suppose your topic is the Iditarod sled dog race. Readers will need to know what the Iditarod is. They also will need to know where

Before you start writing, you must know *why* you are writing. This is your **purpose**. Who are you writing for? What is your topic? Are you writing to explain or compare something?

and when it takes place. You should also explain what makes it important.

A word web is one way to organize information. This is a type of brainstorming. First, make different sections.

They should include Who, What, Where, Why, and How. Then, write down all the details you know. You do not have to use complete sentences.

WORD WEB

WHERE: Alaska.
Anchorage to Nome.

WHO: mushers, dogs, tourists,
sponsors, volunteers.

WHAT: Iditarod

HOW: 1,000 miles, 16 dogs.
9-16 days. Required stops.
Daytime/nighttime run.

WHY: mail, medicine, sled dog
culture, tourism, show off
the dogs.

QUESTIONS
What is the topic of
this word web?
What are some details
the author will include?

CHAPTER TWO

Introductions and Conclusions

Most informational texts are like a hamburger. The first and last paragraphs are the buns. They hold the burger together. Between them are the meat, cheese, and ketchup. These are your details. Without the buns, the other pieces would fall apart. Put together, they make a complete and satisfying text.

The first paragraph is the introduction. It tells your readers what they will learn. The first sentence should grab your readers' attention. This is called a hook. You can begin with a fact that will surprise readers. For example, "Running the Iditarod is so exhausting that people sometimes fall asleep while racing." Or you can begin with a question. For example, "Did you know that sled dogs once saved dozens of children?" If you begin with a question, be sure to answer it later.

If you are explaining something, your transitional words might be *first*, *then*, or *finally*. If you are comparing two things, you might use *similar*, *alike*, and *also*. These transition words tell your reader how two different ideas are connected.

The introduction's next sentences give details. They show what readers will learn. You must explain each detail in later paragraphs. **Transitional words** make sentences easy to follow. These words link ideas and different sentences together.

The introduction also needs a **thesis statement**. This sentence tells readers what they will know after reading your text. For example, you could write, "The Iditarod is an exciting event for many reasons."

Remember the hamburger example? Don't forget the bottom bun! The conclusion is like the introduction. It gives much of the same information. But it does not use the same words. It should restate the most important details.

INTRODUCTION AND CONCLUSION

Introduction

Would you like to race over icy mountains? What if you could do this on a sled with 16 dogs? Hundreds of people do this every year. The Iditarod is a sled dog race in Alaska. The race covers 1,000 miles. It goes over many types of land. The race teaches people about the importance of sled dogs. Racers spend almost a year training their dogs for this dangerous event. The Iditarod is an exciting Alaskan race that takes careful planning.

Conclusion

The Iditarod is a very challenging race. Alaska's wilderness can be dangerous. That means sled dogs must be trained properly. Because of this danger, owners take special care of their dogs. To run a successful race, mushers must think about many things.

QUESTIONS
What is the thesis statement? How are the introduction and conclusion similar?

Body Paragraphs

The body paragraphs are the meat, cheese, and ketchup of your burger. They are the juicy details that your readers will remember. You should have a body paragraph for every detail in your introduction.

Each body paragraph has an important job. It gives a major fact that readers must know. Then it explains why

that fact is important. Finally, it shows an example so readers understand what you mean.

There are other things to think about, too. Make sure that you use good sources. Books, articles, and Web sites should be reliable. If you are writing about the Iditarod, a book about Alaska would be a great source. Also, try to find books that were written in the last few years.

You should not use stories or opinions as sources. Suppose your friend went to Alaska last summer. She might have some great stories. But do not use her stories as a source for your text.

Pictures are very useful. They can help readers understand your information. Include a **caption**, or sentence about the picture. That will help the reader understand the picture's connection to the text.

Rewrite the facts you find. You can use some of the same words. But do not copy the sentences from your source. For example, a book might say, "There are three states of matter, including solids, liquids, and gasses." Do not use the same sentence in your writing. Instead, you might write, "Solids, liquids, and gasses are the three kinds of matter." The sentences mean the same thing. But you wrote it your own way.

Now you know how to write an informational text. It's time to find a topic you like and write about it!

BODY PARAGRAPHS

The Alaskan wilderness has many features that sled teams must face. The race begins in Anchorage and ends in Nome. It lasts for more than 1,000 miles. The sleds must travel over mountains. They must also travel over frozen rivers. Sometimes, the rivers are not frozen. In that case, dogs must go through them. Crossing the tundra can be a challenge, too. No trees grow in the tundra. That means there is nothing to stop the winds. Mushers are the people who guide the dogs. Mushers must train their dogs for these different surfaces.

The musher can use different strategies during the race. For example, will he run his dogs during the day or night? What will he feed his dogs? And how much will he feed them? Also, the dogs must have time to rest. Some mushers take many short breaks. Others go as long as the dogs can last. Then, they take a longer break. These choices can cause a musher to win or lose the race.

QUESTIONS
What is the topic sentence of the second paragraph? What are two details that support the topic? What transitional words do you see?

TIPS FOR YOUNG WRITERS

1. Look at different types of informational texts. What do you notice? How do they help you?

2. Think about things you read in magazines or online. Is the information accurate? How do you know?

3. What interests you? Make a list of questions about the topic, and see if you can find the answers.

4. Where is your favorite place to go? Create a brochure about it. Include details and a picture.

5. Research a time in history that interests you. Write different introductory sentences. Write one surprising fact and one interesting question. Practice writing a hook.

6. Look at different pictures. Write a caption for each.

7. Compare different books on the same topic. Notice the different styles the authors use.

8. Write, write, and write some more. The more you practice, the better you become.

GLOSSARY

body *(BAH-dee):* The body is the information between the introduction and conclusion. The body paragraphs give details about the topic.

caption *(KAP-shun):* A caption is a short explanation of a picture. The caption should provide new information.

conclusion *(kuhn-KLOO-zhun):* A conclusion is the end of a text. The conclusion should restate or summarize important information.

glossary *(GLOS-uh-ree):* A glossary is an alphabetical list that gives the meaning of difficult words in a book. The glossary helps you understand words that you do not know.

index *(IN-deks):* An index is an alphabetical list of subjects at the end of a book, giving the pages on which each subject can be found. Use the index to find a topic.

introduction *(in-truh-DUK-shun):* An introduction is the beginning of a text and lets the reader know what the topic of the text is. The introduction should be interesting to keep the reader's attention.

nonfiction *(non-FIK-shun):* Nonfiction texts are true. A nonfiction text will teach you something that is not made up.

purpose *(PUR-puhs):* A purpose is the reason you do something. The purpose of this book is to teach you to write an informational text.

thesis statement (*THEE-sis STATE-ment*): A thesis statement explains what a text will be about. A thesis statement is an important part of an introduction.

transitional words (*tran-ZISH-un-al WURDS*): Transitional words are words that link ideas together. *First*, *then*, and *last* are examples of transitional words.

TO LEARN MORE

BOOKS

Bree, Loris, and Marlin Bree. *Kid's Trip Diary: Kids! Write about Your Own Adventures and Experiences!* Saint Paul, MN: Marlor Press, Inc., 2007.

Hambleton, Vicki, and Cathleen Greenwood. *So, You Want to Be a Writer? How to Write, Get Published, and Maybe Even Make It Big!* New York: Aladdin/Beyond Words, 2012.

Kinney, Jeff. *The Wimpy Kid Do-It-Yourself Book.* New York: Amulet Books, 2011.

ON THE WEB

Visit our Web site for lots of links about informational texts:
www.childsworld.com/links

Note to Parents, Teachers, and Librarians: We routinely check our Web links to make sure they're safe, active sites—so encourage your readers to check them out!

INDEX

body paragraphs, 5, 16, 20

caption, 18

conclusion, 5, 13, 14

glossary, 5

index, 5

introduction, 5, 11, 12, 13, 14, 16

nonfiction, 4

purpose, 6

sources, 17, 18

thesis statement, 12

transitional words, 12

word web, 6, 8

DATE DUE

PRINTED IN U.S.A.